HOLIDAY HILL

Books by
Edith M. Patch

NATURE STUDY
Dame Bug and Her Babies
Hexapod Stories
Bird Stories
First Lessons in Nature Study
Holiday Pond
Holiday Meadow
Holiday Hill
Holiday Shore
Mountain Neighbors
Desert Neighbors
Forest Neighbors
Prairie Neighbors

NATURE AND SCIENCE READERS
Hunting
Outdoor Visits
Surprises
Through Four Seasons
Science at Home
The Work of Scientists

HOLIDAY HILL

by
Edith M. Patch

Decorations by

Wilfrid S. Bronson

YESTERDAY'S CLASSICS

ITHACA, NEW YORK

This edition, first published in 2020 by Yesterday's Classics, an imprint of Yesterday's Classics, LLC, is an unabridged republication of the text originally published by The MacMillan Company in 1931. For the complete listing of the books that are published by Yesterday's Classics, please visit www.yesterdaysclassics. com. Yesterday's Classics is the publishing arm of Gateway to the Classics which presents the complete text of hundreds of classic books for children at www. gatewaytotheclassics.com.

ISBN: 978-1-63334-049-7

Yesterday's Classics, LLC
PO Box 339
Ithaca, NY 14851

CONTENTS

Holiday Hill

CHAPTER I

THE SIGNS ON THE HILL

DID you ever see a signpost with a mark pointing to a place called "Holiday Hill"? Perhaps not. Yet a holiday hill is not very hard to find. It has certain signs of its own and so it does not need guideboards.

There may be a stream of water running down its steep side. A very little brook will do, if it makes a jolly sound when it splashes against the mossy rocks.

For, of course, there must be rocks on a really satisfying hill. The rocks will have rounded ends and sides, looking as if their corners had been rubbed off. And many of them will have cracks through which bushes are pushing their stems.

If it is really the right sort of hill on which to spend a holiday, it should have berries, don't you think? Of all the berries in the world, those that grow on plants belonging to the Heath Family seem best for a hill.

The stems and leaves of mountain cranberries will lie like a flat mat on the very top of the hill. Their berries will be crimson and as sour as those other cranberries that grow on taller plants in bogs.

1

Blueberry bells waiting for bees

Blueberry bushes will cover part of the slope. Their blossoms will hang like tiny pink and cream-colored bells. Little bees will be going here and there on humming wings, carrying pollen from flower to flower. Because of the visits of these insects during blossom time, there will be berries on the bushes later—beautiful blue berries powdered with wax, sweet in the summer sunshine.

For the third kind of heath plant we might choose to find the checkerberry with leaves that stay green all winter and with red spicy berries that cling to the stems all winter, too, unless they happen to be picked and eaten by some hillside wanderer.

As you climb the slope of Holiday Hill, you may meet Chickaree among a clump of arbor vitae trees. If you do, he will probably scold you, and his voice will sound like his name. But Chickaree will not frighten you for he is only a little red squirrel trying to tell you that he wishes to have all the cones that grow on the evergreen branches for his own.

Sir Talis will not frighten you, either, if you are a sensible person. For Sir Talis is a harmless creature, gliding out of sight among the rocks in a quiet well-mannered way.

The small being in a strange cloak, who sits on a sweet fern bush and munches its fragrant leaves, will fill you with curiosity, I think. He did me, the first time I met him.

If you hear a springtime song like a soft tinkling of gentle bells, you may suspect that Junco is near. When he flies, he will show you the white outer feathers of his spread tail.

During the fall of the year, you may take the colors of Holiday Hill for a sign that you have reached the right place. For then there will be gay leaves of crimson shades and some of gleaming gold.

But if you wait until winter, what will the hillside

be, then, except a pleasant slope for coasting? Well, if you are lucky enough, you may chance to see the tracks that Little Snowshoes made when he passed that way. And, if you are much more fortunate still, you may even have a glimpse of the little fellow himself—all snug in his white winter furs.

So, springtime or summer or autumn or winter, you may know "Holiday Hill" when you climb it, even though there is no guidepost to tell you its name.

CHAPTER II

THE OLD BOULDER

THE granite rocks with rounded corners that sit on Holiday Hill year after year seem like idle things. They have a settled look as if they had been there always and would stay forever.

That giant stone, the biggest one of them all—what has it ever done? On a hot summer day, it casts a shadow where children can play comfortably or where they can sit and read without the glare of sunshine in their eyes. On blustery days, the wind breaks against the rock, leaving a quiet place on one side of it.

Perhaps you may think that is enough for a great rock to do, to make a pleasant shelter from sun and wind. What else, indeed, can it ever have done than just sit still? You will feel better acquainted with Holiday Hill itself, I think, if you know something about that huge piece of granite which looks so steadfast and unchangeable.

For the old boulder has a story of its own quite as marvelous as the tale of anything else on the hill. And in spite of the rock's quiet way of sitting there, its story is one of travel and adventure and mystery.

The mystery was a matter that kept many wise men guessing for many years.

Granite rocks with rounded corners

Vast numbers of such boulders, large and small, may be found in different places all over the northeastern part of North America. And wherever they are, there are reasons to think that they have been brought from somewhere else.

For such boulders are quite likely to be some kind of rock that is different from the solid bedrock that lies under the soil in which the boulders rest. In many places the bedrock is limestone and yet the boulders, big and little, may be granite like those of Holiday Hill.

Although they are different from the bedrock of their locality, they are like the bedrock in some other region, often far away. Certain granite boulders are like the granite mountain tops a hundred miles or more distant.

Indeed, the boulders and the mountains are so much alike that men who studied them came to think that the boulders had been broken off the mountains and scattered about the country for many miles.

The shape of the boulders puzzled people, too. They are so much like huge pebbles with their rounded sides and ends.

Of course it is easy to understand why pebbles which are touched by moving water are without sharp corners. If they are on the seashore the waves splash over them and rub them together until they become smoother and smoother. And if the little stones are in the bed of a river they are pushed against one another by the swift water currents and their rough edges are rubbed down.

But how had the great heavy rocks, in the soil or on top of it, come to be similar in shape to the little stones in rivers and on the seashore? How had their corners been worn off?

The longer people studied boulders, the more they came to believe that the large rocks had their blunt edges, as the pebbles had, by being pushed against some hard objects. It was because they thought these big stones had been knocked or rolled or bowled from one place to another that they gave them the name of boulders.

You can see what a mystery this was. What could have broken the rocky tops of mountains? What could have carried the broken pieces of rock about the country and dropped them here and there?

At last a man found an answer to these questions. His name was Louis Agassiz. In another country he had seen some high rocky mountains that were covered by enormous, deep masses of ice and snow. He knew what happened when great bodies of ice, called glaciers, pushed slowly down the mountains.

Louis Agassiz knew, too, what such a glacier did while it moved. It broke off parts of the rocks beneath it. The rocks became embedded in the ice and were carried with it. A glacier was like a solid river of ice, hundreds of feet deep, pushing rocks and soil as it went slowly on its way. And as the ice melted, of course the embedded stones dropped to the ground beneath.

It seemed to Louis Agassiz that the boulders and much of the soil in the northeastern part of North America looked like boulders and soil that had been carried by glaciers and dropped as the ice melted.

So he believed that once, long, long ago, the mountains in this part of our country were covered with enormous weights of ice and snow. He reasoned that glaciers from these must have pushed across the

A glacier is a slow-moving river of ice.

land, grinding off the hilltops, broadening the valleys and shoving rocks and soil from place to place. Then, finally, as the ice melted, the boulders were left wherever they chanced to drop.

The more men thought about what Louis Agassiz told them of the movements of glaciers, the more reasonable his answer to the boulder mystery seemed. And now you may find in certain books, accounts of how the travel-worn boulders were carried by moving ice.

9

So we understand that the ancient stone on Holiday Hill is one of many that came from some far mountain. After a long and remarkable journey, it was left there a stranger.

But the boulder is not a stranger, now. It has sat on the same hillside for no one knows how many hundreds of years, and it seems quite at home there.

Though its travels were over long ago, its adventures were not, for changes came to the old boulder of Holiday Hill from year to year.

Air and moisture acted upon the surface of the rock, season by season, crumbling bits of it somewhat as iron is rusted when left outdoors.

Rain and snow fell upon the stone and settled in its hollows. When the water froze in winter, the rock was cracked in places.

Dust and brown dry leaves were blown upon the boulder. Some of these were later washed into the cracks by rain and formed tiny beds of soil.

Seeds, brought by wind or birds or squirrels, fell on this soil and grew. The roots of the plants reached into the cracks and pushed as far as they could into the crumbled spots.

Fires swept over that part of the hill, burning dry leaves and woody stems and tree trunks and leaving ashes and charcoal near the boulder and blackening its sides with smoke. Perhaps lightning had started some of the fires. Perhaps others had spread from Indian camps.

Plants grew on the hillside that had been cleared

by fires. They scattered their seeds and spread their roots until in time the black ground was hidden under green leaves.

There were other plants of a quite different sort touching the boulder. They spread like a mat over the rock and covered much of its surface. These were the greenish gray lichens that lay with their flat parts so close against the rock that it was hard to tell where lichen left off and stone began.

Lichens had been living on Holiday Boulder ever since some tiny spores from lichens on other rocks had floated through the air and settled on this one.

The spores were finer than dust you can see in the air, but they were not too small to hold life. Young lichens grew from them, as some other plants start from seeds. The lichens had acid in them that softened the surface in which they grew. So they were able to get a firmer and firmer hold on the particles of rock to which they clung. They gave the rounded sides of the great stone a soft and lovely color.

One plant grew from a crevice in the very top of the boulder. It was a very large plant to be growing out of so narrow a crack. It was, indeed, a pine tree nearly twenty feet tall, and it was old enough to have cones with seeds.

Had that pine tree sprouted from a seed that had been blown to the top of the boulder years ago? Or had a bird perched there and dropped it? Or had a squirrel chosen that crack for a pantry and filled it with pine seeds, one of which had sprouted and grown?

*Lichens covered the sides of Holiday Boulder and
a pine tree grew in a crack at its top.*

You may ask that old giant rock as many questions as you like. But Holiday Boulder will be silent. It has no memory of any pine seed that was placed in its crevice. It does not feel the roots of the tree that are even now crowding against the sides of the crack. It does not know that blueberry bushes are brushing its surface with their branches and pushing their stems through its crumbling granite base. It does not feel the touch of the acid lichens or sense the difference between fire and frost.

12

Yes, you may question that ancient stone; but it has no knowledge of any of the events in all the marvelous story of its existence. Not even of that strange and icy journey that took place during those years before it came to sit on Holiday Hill!

CHAPTER III

HEATH BELLS AND BERRIES

HEATH is a name for open uncultivated land. Many kinds of plants cannot live on certain heaths. The soil is not right for them. Other plants, however, thrive in such ground. Indeed, one family of plants is called "Heath Family" because so many of its members grow on heaths.

Blueberries belong to the Heath Family. As you already know, there are blueberries growing on Holiday Hill. Some of them, which are close to the old stones, are neighborly enough to reach through cracks in the crumbling granite.

There are blueberry bushes growing away from the rocks, too. Their roots have run in all directions until one whole slope of the hill is covered with them.

No man planted these blueberry bushes. They were growing there long before any man found them. For many years the berries were picked and the seeds were scattered without any help from people.

Bears and smaller furry animals, with a fondness for sweet fruit, had countless pleasant picnics on the sunny hillside.

Sometimes gulls flew away from the sea and the shore to the hill where they gathered blueberries for a change. Fruit-eating song birds came often to feast there.

Doubtless both the furry and the feathered berry-pickers scattered seeds here and there; and doubtless some of these seeds grew to make more bushes. But, except for such seeds as they chanced to drop, animals of those sorts could do little to aid the blueberry plants.

Blueberry bushes pushed their stems through cracks in the crumbling granite.

But there were certain other animals that helped in a different and more important way. These were the insects that hovered over the heath while the blossoms dangled like little pink and creamy bells.

Among the visiting insects, none were more abundant and useful than bees. For bees flew to the bushes to drink the sweet nectar they found in the blossoms; and while they were sipping nectar they did a good deed to the plants that fed them. The service which bees and some other insect guests performed was to carry pollen from blossom to blossom.

Each blueberry flower needed pollen from another blueberry flower to enable its juicy fruit and its seeds to grow. Wind could not carry the pollen for them and drop it into the nodding bell-shaped heath blossoms. Nothing could help these plants in this way except the insects. Such heath plants and insects have lived together for ages. They need each other.

Of course these insects never knew they were helping the blueberries. They simply felt thirsty for nectar and went to the blossoms to drink.

When a visiting bee thrust her strong tongue up into a blueberry blossom, she moved the parts inside that held the pollen. The golden dust poured down upon her and stuck to her body. Then when she reached another blossom and brushed against its moist sticky stigma, some of the pollen came off her body and stayed on the stigma.

All through blossom time thousands of bees have

been carrying their dusty loads of pollen year after year. But, of course, the birds and the beasts have never known that they had little insects to thank for all the sweet juicy berries they picked on the hillside!

The open blueberry slope of Holiday Hill once had trees growing on it so close together that but little sunlight could get through their branches. Some of these trees were cut and some were burned by white men. It is quite likely that some were burned by Indians before that. And perhaps lightning may have set some blazing fires that spread over the hillside.

Lightning may have set some blazing fires.

No place could have been more inviting to blueberry bushes than such sunny land free from overhanging branches. Their roots and underground stems reached into the soil that had been cleared by fires. More and more new bushes sprouted from the old ones until, after a long time, these plants covered most of the ground that had once been shaded by trees.

It has been several years since a bear was seen on Holiday Hill, though certain smaller furry animals still come and go. So do birds with a liking for good sweet fruit. Their happy chirps may be heard from time to time.

There is another cheerful sound, too, that often floats about the hillside nowadays. The laughter of children is in the air—children with berry-stained fingers and faces.

Bearberry blossoms are bell-like.

Even though they spend much of their time among the blueberries, they find other plants of the Heath Family, too.

Bearberry shrubs with trailing stems grow in rocky places. Their red fruits are pretty to look at, but the children do not find them good to eat.

Another member of the Heath Family grows well in the granite gravel on the hillside. Spicy red checkerberries may be found on this plant almost any time of year. They have a pleasant flavor in the late summer before they are full-grown. They stay on the plant all winter and are still good early the next summer when they are nearly a year old. These berries are firmer than blueberries and not so juicy.

Checkerberry plants, too, have insects to thank for all their seeds. And no animal could enjoy the rosy fruit if it were not for the little pollen-bearers.

Of course the feathered and furry berry-pickers do not know about heath blossoms and insects. Children, however, are wiser and can learn to think thankfully of little wild bees whenever they gather tasty heath berries.

But the fruit is not the only good-flavored part of a checkerberry plant. When the leaves are young and tender, they are quite as good as the berries to eat. The leaves are fragrant. "Aromatic" is the word that a botanist uses when he speaks of checkerberry leaves.

That is a pleasant-sounding word for spicy leaves. Wintergreen is another name for a checkerberry. That is a good name for it, as its leaves stay green all winter.

19

Checkerberry, or wintergreen, or teaberry

You do not really need to eat checkerberry leaves or fruit to learn about wintergreen flavor. You can find out, if you wish, by eating certain kinds of candy.

But, of course, it is much pleasanter to visit the plants themselves. And while you are there on Holiday Hill, you may like to think that once long ago some Indians climbed that slope and found the same kind of heath plants growing.

For Indians used to gather the aromatic wintergreen leaves and steep them in hot water for tea. And if you wish to learn how that sort of drink tastes, why not make some for yourself? As you sip it you may be interested to know that this member of the Heath Family has still another name and is sometimes called teaberry.

CHAPTER IV

THE CONE HUNT

CHICKAREE's name rhymed with Chickadee, and while he was quite young he stayed in a nest. But, for all that, Chickaree was not a bird. He was a squirrel.

The nest where Chickaree and his brothers and sisters lived their first spring was near the top of a ragged old pine on one side of Holiday Hill. After the young squirrels could climb and run they had many frolics among the branches of this tree. They played hide-and-seek and tag, and they chattered most gayly. Now and then they returned to their big dry nest of brown leaves and shredded bark to rest. If their mother were at home, they cuddled beside her.

There came a time, however, when these brothers and sisters were old enough to leave the house and lot that belonged to their father and mother and take care of themselves.

Chickaree chose Arbor Vitae Camp for his own new home.

Arbor vitae trees often grow in low swampy places; but hillsides are all right for them, too, especially if their roots can find plenty of moisture. Arbor Vitae Camp is about halfway up Holiday Hill. A little brook runs down that side of the hill, and the tall trees as well as the short plants growing there are different from many of those on drier and more open parts of the hill.

Arbor Vitae Camp

It is a gurgling, burbling sort of brook, making tiny waterfalls as it leaps over bits of broken granite here and there. Chickaree, being a talkative and jumping young creature, quite possibly found some companionship in the music and the motions of the brook.

Of course Chickaree could not pay money for Arbor Vitae Camp and get a deed for it. He could not put up a sign with the words NO TRESPASSING on it. But before he was quite a year old he had some perfectly good squirrel ways of telling the wild world that he owned the place.

He stood on a branch and sang. His early spring tune was a series of pleasing notes that churred and rolled in happy tones. Fond as he was of music, he would sing nothing except his own solos.

If other squirrels tried to stay too near, he never sang any male duets or trios or quartets with them. Indeed, at such times, he stopped singing altogether and began to scold. If the other squirrels did not understand that he meant what he said, he chased them. And if that was not enough of a hint for them to go away from Arbor Vitae Camp, he fought—and his teeth were very sharp.

You may think from these actions that Chickaree had rather ugly manners. But it is well to consider that he had no gate that he could close. He had no lock and key. There was no policeman to walk back and forth and help protect his property. And there were many other places for other squirrels.

There was, however, one squirrel whom he did not chase or scold. She did not disturb his happy spring song. She liked his voice, and he seemed to enjoy singing to her. In fact, he actually invited her to stay and share his home. She accepted the invitation and became Mrs. Chickaree.

Mr. and Mrs. Chickaree were especially handsome in their spring colors, which were brighter than those they had been wearing. They lost their rather dingy, rusty look when winter was over. The ruddy back fur was separated from the white under fur by a neat dark line along each side. Their fluffy red tails had a prettier glow, too, for a while. Their fresh suits were becoming to them.

Mrs. Chickaree could not spend much of her time listening to squirrel songs. She found that a family of five youngsters kept her rather busy. As she was so very fond of them all, there was nothing she would rather do than take care of them. She was quite happy most of the time though she had a worried day when something happened to the nest and she had to move her family one at a time.

Each baby reached up its arms and held its little hands around its mother's neck while she carried it to a safer place. They could use their front paws like hands in so many ways that it seems natural to speak of them by that name.

Daddy Chickaree did not spend much time singing, as summer came on. He guarded his family and premises like a little watch dog, barking at all intruders. He even tried to scare away big creatures like the children from Holiday Farm.

At such times he barked so fast and furiously that he seemed to be coughing and sneezing and growling and squealing all at once. For his voice had low tones and high tones, and the queer thing about it was that he sounded as if he were using all his tones at the same moment.

When he ran out on a branch in a threatening way, his little face had a very cross expression, and his tail jerked and twitched with his fierce excitement.

But all his efforts were wasted on the children, for they were not a bit frightened. They only laughed. His fury, somehow, seemed just funny to them. They told him politely that they liked to come to the shade of Arbor Vitae Camp now and then, but they would not harm him or his family or take away the food from his

Young Chickaree and two of his brothers

pantry. And by way of peace offering, they often left a few peanuts where Chickaree could find them.

Chickaree did not understand the words they said to him, but he did seem to comprehend the message of the peanuts. So, as time went on, he did not scold them nearly as terribly as he had done at first.

Food interested Chickaree greatly, of course. What he ate was important to him, as, indeed, it must be to all animals. He found variety enough quite near his home.

He liked fruit and enjoyed the juicy sweet blueberries

Food interested Chickaree greatly.

on the hillside. He needed some meat, too, and caught grasshoppers and other insects which he found here and there. Eggs and tender young fowl tasted good to him and, if he could find them in birds' nests, he helped himself. He was that kind of hunter.

Chickaree was a hunter.

Of course such a hunting trip was a sad affair for the birds who built the nests and laid the eggs. It is easy to see why Chickaree and his family were most unpopular with the birds of Holiday Hill. That may be the reason why so few of them chose to have their nests near Arbor Vitae Camp.

Seeds of many sorts pleased Chickaree, and perhaps there were none he liked better than those that grow in cones. The first seeds of this kind he had ever eaten came out of pine cones on his father's lot, where he lived when he was younger. He had once found some spruce seeds that he had been glad to eat. But the arbor vitae seeds that grew in his own camp satisfied him, too.

Since squirrels do not spend their winters in sleep, as woodchucks and frogs and some other animals do, Chickaree needed to have food stored for winter use. There would be cold days when Holiday Hill would be covered with snow. He must have plenty of food in piles where he could find it easily.

It seems unlikely that Chickaree could have done much real thinking about winter while all his hillside world was green and summery. So perhaps he gathered food for the mere fun of doing it. Certainly, while he was picking his cones, he acted as if there were nothing quite so jolly as a good cone hunt. He seemed never to be too tired, although he worked busily most of the day from sunrise to sunset.

He began to harvest his crop about the first of September. The trees were loaded with cones as that year was one of heavy bearing. To be sure the cones were not ripe yet. They were still almost cream-colored and were tinted with very pale green. Their scales were tightly closed, and the seeds were all safe inside.

These little cones do not grow singly like spruce or fir or pine cones. Arbor vitae leaves lie in flat sprays, and the tips of the branches spread out like open fans.

The cones grow in clusters near the ends of the sprays. Often there are fifty or more cones in such a cluster.

Do you think that Chickaree cut those tiny cones one by one? Not at all! He nipped the twig with his teeth so that the whole end fell together. By the time he was through with a branch, all its tips were well trimmed.

A cone cluster cut by Chickaree

His pruning shears were good tools. He could work very fast with them. They never became rusty or in need of sharpening. Snip, snip, snip—and down came a shower of cones! This was a jolly way to harvest a crop.

For several days Chickaree left the cones where they fell. It seemed to be more important for him to cut them than to gather them. If they stayed on the trees too long they would ripen and the seeds would drop out. His motto seemed to be "Hurry, hurry, hurry, lest a seed get lost!"

By the end of the first week in September the cone clusters lay on the ground in thick circles around the trees. Then the busy squirrel began to put his cone food away for winter.

What sort of places do you think Chickaree chose for this harvest? Good dry pantries like hollows in old trees or little caves sheltered by rock roofs? Not at all. He put his cones into cool damp places. He used cold storage for them.

Chickaree dug some small holes in soggy moss where the brook kept the ground wet. He did this with a few quick movements of his strong little hands. Into such a hole he tucked only a few cone clusters or often only one.

Most of the crop, however, he stored in large open cellars that he did not need to dig. He found some wet mossy hollows shaded by the trees and filled them; and he piled many cones between two old logs.

The cousins from Holiday Farm found these cellars, and Uncle David permitted them to measure one. The clusters lay in a heap about fifteen inches long, ten inches wide and four inches deep. There were more than three hundred clusters of cones in this heap. As most of the clusters had fifty or more cones, you can see there would be a great many arbor vitae seeds there even if each cone held only ten good seeds. There were probably somewhat more than $300 \times 50 \times 10$ seeds in that one cellar of Chickaree's!

Another cellar had a larger heap—much larger. It looked more than five times as large. But the children did not touch this one to measure it or to count the seeds. Chickaree came and scolded them severely. He was very much worried about it. He had worked so long to cut all those cones and pack them away in flat piles that it is not strange he was anxious to keep them safe. The cousins thought they might feel as he did if they had harvested the cones.

Chickaree had been busy every day for about three weeks cutting and storing his crop of cones. He had done his work at exactly the right time. By the last week in September the season of unripe arbor vitae cones was over. There were only a few left on the trees in Chickaree's camp, and most of these had opened their scales. At a touch their seeds scattered to the ground.

But Chickaree's seeds not did scatter. The closed cones stored in his damp cellars did not open. Neither did they become sour or moldy. Perhaps there was enough aromatic cedar oil in the cones to keep them well preserved. Even those that were left untouched until the next spring were fresh and good.

The Chickaree family had their winter home in a dry hollow in an old tree. They slept there at night, each with a long tail curled around for a fur cover. During the very coldest, stormiest days they felt dozy and stayed at home then, too.

They were awake and active, however, on pleasant winter days. They were hungry, too. That is why the heaps of cones in Chickaree's cellars became smaller and smaller as time went on.

Little tunnels under the snow led, like subways, into these cellars. And here and there a pile of cone scales showed where a squirrel had brought his cones to nibble and break them for his dinner of seeds.

So the squirrel's cone hunt was not only a pleasant September task. It served, too, to provide food during a long cold winter when there were no berries or insects to be found.

In this connection it is interesting to know that the name "arbor vitae" means "tree of life." Chickaree never learned the meaning of those words. But he seemed, nevertheless, to appreciate the trees and their cones.

CHAPTER V

A TUFT OF EVENING PRIMROSES

It was moonlight on Holiday Hill. The light was bright for night-time, as the moon was full. By it could be seen a well worn path that led up one side of the hill.

The odors of flowers drifted across the slope, some of them far sweeter than they ever were by day.

A quivery, quavery sound came through the quiet air. Somewhere out in the night an owl was calling—or perhaps it was a raccoon. The voices of some owls are so much like those of raccoons that it is often hard to tell the difference.

Moonlight, fragrance, strange musical notes—all seemed like invitations to pleasant and interesting experiences that can never be met during daytime hours. Anyone accepting them could have something better than dreams to remember by following the beaten track that lay between the meadow and the old hedgerow.

The plants beside the path had strange night manners. Clovers had folded their leaves. Dandelions

Holiday Hill by moonlight

had hidden their golden heads. They seemed to be resting. Bees and butterflies that sought flowers during the sunny hours were not there at night. They, too, were resting. Indeed, the whole daytime world seemed to be asleep.

But the night creatures were awake. There was a sound of some small animal moving among the bushes in the hedgerow. Several bats were flying overhead. A little owl drifted by on silent wings. A moment later he gave a sweet shivery call. Another owl answered him from a distance.

Even children who went often up the hill in the daytime, and were most familiar with it then, would have stopped in amazement halfway up the sloping path. For in the summer night, the trail led to a world of strange surprises.

A wave of fragrance passed across it—a scent sweeter than any the day breezes ever brought the place. And all around were wide-flaring flowers. They were on tall plants that, during the day, looked like big wilty weeds slouching in the sunshine.

But now these evening primroses were at their loveliest. Their stalks stood alert. Their dew-drenched leaves were fresh. Their pale yellow petals opened into blossoms that were marvelously beautiful.

Suddenly there was a whirring sound of wings as if a humming bird had come. And there, hovering before the very nearest flowers was a creature about the size and somewhat the shape of a humming bird. Like a humming bird, too, it poised before one flower and then another to sip the nectar it found.

Of course a humming bird would have been asleep. This was not a bird of any sort. It was a beautiful insect named, because of its appearance, a humming-bird moth.

A humming-bird moth

The wide-open, gleaming blossoms and the heavy fragrance of the evening primroses might seem strange and wonderful to a human being who usually walked that path in the daytime. But they did not surprise the moth. The light and odor of these flowers were a part of the life of the large insect. It, and others of its kind, visited evening primroses every pleasant night at this season of the year.

The large bird-shaped insect drank nectar and departed. A second visitor, however, stayed with the plants. She was a moth, also, though a small one with fringes on her wings. She was, indeed, so very, very small that a good name for her is Tiny. This wee mother had an important errand that night. She had some eggs to lay and she must put them in just the right places.

The baby caterpillars that were going to hatch from those eggs would need a special sort of diet. They would have such dainty appetites that nothing would agree with them except the tender parts that are found inside the buds of evening primroses. So, of course, the mother moth placed her eggs near the favorite food of her young. That was all she could ever do for them.

She is likely to be far away before it is time for one of her caterpillar brood to hatch. The young larva, however, does not need to find its mother. It makes itself comfortable inside a bud and feasts on stamens with lobes of stigma for a side-dish.

Now, as you know, plants grow stigmas and stamens for purposes of their own. That is their normal way of providing for the seed-children. So a primrose bud that has had its most important parts nibbled out may quite as well not waste its energy in blossoming.

But the fluids of growth pour into such a bud as they do into the others that are whole and sound. The bud responds—not by opening its petals and being a flower, but by staying closed and growing fat and chunky until it is just the sort of cozy nursery to hold a young caterpillar.

So, when you look at a bud of an evening primrose, you can tell by its shape whether a caterpillar has been living inside it. If the bud is long and slender, it should open some evening into a beautiful and fragrant flower. But if it is short and plump, a blossom will never come out of it though something else may.

For there will be a time when the little rascal inside has eaten its fill and must leave. It chews a round doorway through the side of the bud for its escape. Next it spins a filmy cocoon of silk. Within this dainty sleeping bag it changes first to a pupa. A fortnight or so later the pupa, in turn, changes to a sprite of a fringe-winged moth like Tiny, its mother.

A moth of a third kind often visits the evening primrose. Her first name is rather long; but her second name is Florida, so we will call her that.[1] Florida's beautiful wings measure a little less than an inch and a quarter across when they are spread wide open. They are pink with pale yellow borders. Like the big humming-bird moth, this lovely creature seeks the blossoms to

---

[1] Her full name is *Rhodophora florida.* Of course you may use it all, if you prefer.

drink sweet nectar. Like Tiny, with the fringy wings, she comes to lay her eggs.

The young caterpillars which hatch from her eggs are green. At first they nibble holes in the tender buds. When they are older, they cling to the unripe seed-pods, the color of which matches the green of their bodies.

During the day the caterpillars rest among the seed pods so quietly that even keen-eyed and hungry birds may not notice them, although they are in plain sight. But when night comes they are awake and active. They bite into the juicy pods filled with seeds that seem as tempting to their taste as green peas are to ours. Before morning comes they have eaten so much that they can rest all day without being too hungry.

Florida, the mother with the rosy and yellow wings, sips nectar from dusk to dawn or busies herself during the night with her eggs that need to be laid. She, also, hides on the plant while she takes her daytime nap. She does not stay among the seed pods with her green caterpillar family, however. She seeks a nook more in harmony with her own colors.

The primrose flowers that were open a night or two before hang with drooping petals in the sunlight. The yellow blossoms, in fading, have become somewhat pinkish inside. The sleepy moth creeps into one of these chambers, pink-lined and yellow-edged. The yellow borders of her pink wings reach a little beyond the petal tips.

If you think Florida will be easy to find when she is napping, go and hunt for her some day!

Fortunately for evening primroses, they have so many seeds that some can be spared to the hungry caterpillars that will grow to be lovely moths. There will be seeds for birds to eat, too, and even then there will be enough left to be scattered on the ground by the winds.

A plant that sprouts from one of these seeds does not grow to be tall during its first season. It spends that time spreading a rosette of leaves flat on the ground.

All the soil under this round mat belongs to the seedling primrose. That is the way it has of claiming its own home. Other plants cannot thrive in the shade under the thick leaves; and so the primrose has room for its own roots.

Over-wintering rosette of evening primrose

The young plant passes its first winter as a circular tuft of leaves. In the spring it is ready to send up a tall central stem. When summer comes this is tipped with yellow flowers most fragrant and lovely at night.

Although evening primroses grow near the tops of rather high hills, they grow also in low places. They are so common that you cannot go far in most country places without passing some of them.

Perhaps you have seen them only on some sunshiny day when their stems seemed weak, their leaves were limp, and their flowers were drooping. It may be that even their scent was stale and feeble. But it is not fair to judge an evening primrose by the way it looks in the daytime.

Evening primroses, of course, should be visited at night, as you can tell by their name. It is not necessary to wait until very late, however. The two pictures opposite were both taken of the same plant one evening shortly after eight o'clock. The second photograph was taken ten minutes later than the first. Who would not like to see so many petals fly open in ten minutes?

It was Margaret Deland who told how children came

> To watch the primrose blow. Silent they stood,
>   Hand clasped in hand, in breathless hush around,
> And saw her shyly doff her soft green hood
>   And blossom—with a silken burst of sound.

And John Keats knew, too,

>   A tuft of evening primroses
> O'er which the wind may hover till it dozes;
> O'er which it well might take a pleasant sleep,
> But that 'tis ever startled by the leap
> Of buds into ripe flowers.

Only one flower was open at five minutes after eight.

Seven flowers were open at fifteen minutes after eight.

Surely with the speech of poets in our ears, it would be unbecoming of me to tell you in prose how these blossoms open.

After all, why should you be told? For those of you who live anywhere from Labrador to the Gulf of Mexico and east of the Rocky Mountains are likely to be near enough a wild plant of this sort to go and see for yourselves how it is done. Those who dwell in other places can, perhaps, visit a garden variety which will serve the purpose as well.

CHAPTER VI

A STRANGE CLOAK

MANY years ago men often wore sleeveless cloaks or mantles. These garments were long and loose. They were open in front so that the men who wore them could use their arms easily. A Greek name for such a mantle is *chlamys*.

It has long been a custom of people who study plants and animals to give them Greek names. The name of the small animal in this story is Chlamys. He was called Chlamys because he wore a strange cloak or mantle.

Like the mantles the old Greeks wore, the cloak of little Chlamys was open in front. He thrust his head and his six legs out through this opening and held his cloak over the rest of his body.

If you had met Chlamys walking along Sweet Fern Lane, you might have mistaken him for a very tiny snail. For his mantle was not soft like a piece of cloth but stiff and shell-like. And, although he traveled on six small feet instead of one large foot, his motions seemed somewhat like those of a snail as he went across a leaf.

When Chlamys was disturbed, he had a habit of drawing his head and feet into his mantle. As there was then nothing to hold him to the leaf, he rolled off and fell to the ground.

That was an excellent place for him to hide. He would lie there looking like a little brown pellet among the bits of brown leafy loam under the sweet fern branches. Not even a keen-eyed bird was likely to find him in such a hiding place. He was lost to everything except himself! When all seemed quiet again, out would come his head and six feet, and Chlamys would climb the sweet fern bush and eat a fresh tender leaf for a salad.

In spite of his snail-like manners of carrying his shelter wherever he went, and of pulling himself safely inside when he was touched, Chlamys was not a snail. As of course you know, no snail ever traveled on six feet. He was, indeed, an infant beetle.

Certain young insects make little coverings in which they live while they are in their early stages. Such

The mother of Chlamys

insects are called "case-bearers" because they carry, or bear, their mantles or cases. When they become grown insects with wings, they put aside these little things and leave them empty like garments that have been thrown away.

Perhaps Chlamys would have eaten certain other kinds of leaves if his mother had put the egg from which he hatched on another sort of bush. Beetles of this species are said to like the leaves of raspberry and blackberry and some other plants. But certainly there is no flavor they like better than that of the sweet fern.

You cannot always tell, by its name, what a thing really is. An oak-apple is not an apple but a large round gall caused by an insect. A high-bush cranberry is not a cranberry but a sour red fruit that grows on a plant closely related to a snowball bush. A guinea pig is not a pig but a cavy. And a sweet fern is not a fern but a bush belonging to the Sweet Gale Family.

Plants that belong to the same family are alike in some ways. Near Holiday Farm there were three kinds of plants of the Sweet Gale Family, and they all had fragrant leaves. One of these was the sweet gale shrub that grew on low boggy ground at one side of Holiday Pond. Another was the bayberry that lived within sight of the sea at Holiday Cove. And the third kind was the sweet fern that thrived on Holiday Hill. The flowers of these three plants grow in catkins. Their fruits are small and dry and nutlike.

Sweet gale flower-catkins come in spring before the leaves are out. If they are boiled, a fragrant wax may be obtained from them. The fruit is covered with particles of wax. In some countries candles have been made from sweet gale wax. Parts of the plant may be used to color different things. Indians, in Canada, liked to use the catkin buds to dye their porcupine quills.

The aromatic wax of the bayberry is more abundant than that of the sweet gale shrub. It forms a rather thick coating over the dry fruit. Even in these days, when paraffin candles are so common, people still make candles of bayberry wax. Perhaps you have had dull green, tapering candles, called "bayberry dips," to burn at Christmas time. When you blow out the light of such a candle, the room is filled with its fragrance. Another name for this shrub and its fruit is candleberry.

Sweet fern shrubs grew in great numbers on Holiday Hill. Indeed, there were so many of them on parts of the hill among the blueberries that they were looked upon as weeds. They shaded the lower bushes too much; and their roots and underground stems crowded those of other plants that were near them. Men sometimes came up from the farm and tore out these bushes to give the blueberries a better chance to grow.

In many places on the hill, however, the sweet ferns were permitted to stay year after year. Some children had a path through them which they called "Sweet Fern Lane." They loved to go along this path because of the spicy scent that filled the air when they brushed against the leaves and bruised them.

Some one told them that Indians used to gather sweet fern leaves for pillows. So the children made

Overhanging Sweet Fern Lane

little pillows filled with the fragrant leaves and catkins.

Quite possibly the mother of Chlamys liked the scent of sweet fern as well as people do. Perhaps it had even a stronger attraction for her. It may be that one day when she smelled it she could not keep away from it.

However it came about, this much is certain—the mother beetle put her eggs on the plant that would furnish food for her young. Six-footed mothers have a way of laying their eggs in places that will make good homes for their larval infants; and, of course, the mother of Chlamys was no exception to this rule.

47

She was a pretty beetle a little more than an eighth of an inch long. Her colors were green and bronze. The wing-covers, that lay like a curved shield over her back when they were closed, had many tiny humps on them. She glistened like polished metal and looked like an ornament. She would have made a beautiful model for a decoration on a bronze vase.

When anything came too near her, she hid in a way that is called "playing 'possum." Whenever an opossum is afraid, it lies absolutely still as if it were not alive. Most animals in their natural homes are not easily seen unless they are moving. Keeping quiet is one of their best ways of hiding. Animals that do this are said to be "playing 'possum." This habit is also called "freezing," because the animals are stiff and still as if they were frozen.

When she let go of the leaf she rolled off; but she did not even wiggle when she hit the ground. She lay without a motion in the leafy rubbish there. She could not have been any quieter if she had fainted. After a while she crept out of her hiding place; but by that time everything was calm again.

Being so small, herself, you could hardly expect her eggs to be much bigger than specks. I doubt if you could find one without a magnifying glass.

And, of course, the baby Chlamys that hatched from one of her eggs was a tiny creature to begin with. Tiny but capable! Soon after eating his first few sweet fern salads, he had made a little cloak for himself. He made it the right size, too. Think of that! A mere baby beetle could fasten little brown bits together with a sort of gluey silk until he had a mantle that exactly fitted him!

As fast as he grew he added more brown bits to his cloak, so it was always big enough to cover him. He did not need a new one, because he could piece the old one. It did not look as if it had been made of scraps, however, and its edges were always tidy.

All the time Chlamys was a growing larva he had the protection of his cloak. After he had eaten all the sweet fern salads he could hold, he was ready for a rather long rest. But he did not leave his cloak while he took his nap. He fastened it to a twig of sweet fern and closed the opening.

During his sleep, the little mantle, or sac, served as a sort of cocoon. He had stopped being a growing larva. He was not yet a winged beetle. He was now in the stage between a larva and an adult insect. He was a pupa. While an insect is a pupa many changes take place in its body. It loses the legs and mouth and skin it has had from the beginning, and new parts are formed. Its shape is changed in many ways. And its wings grow.

So, when Chlamys woke, he was a different-looking creature altogether. Instead of being a fat little grub, he had become a fully grown beetle a bit more than an eighth of an inch long. Like his mother before him, he looked like a little metal ornament. If some artist wished to find a good model for a decoration on a bronze vase, what better shape could he find than Chlamys?

CHAPTER VII

SIR TALIS

A WISE man said, long, long ago, that the way of a serpent upon a rock was too wonderful for him to know.

So when you meet Sir Talis you need not be ashamed if there are many wonderful things about him that you do not know. He may seem a bit mysterious to you as he glides out of sight.

This much you will know, of course—that you need never fear Sir Talis; for he is a peaceful garter snake with no harm in him for any man, woman, or child. He is a quite gentlemanly fellow who attends only to his own affairs.

Years ago, when noblemen wore silk and velvet clothes of rich and lovely colors, their garters were gay-striped ribbons. There is an ancient Order of the Garter having princes and knights for members. The badge of this Order is a velvet ribbon edged with gold.

If you look at Sir Talis with friendly eyes, you may perhaps be reminded of a ribbon striped with gold. For, along the middle of his back and low on each side, there is a yellow stripe running from head to tail.

Since the name of this graceful snake is written in learned books with sir to begin it, we may, perhaps, be excused if we speak of his father and mother as Sir and Lady Garter.

The mother of Sir Talis

These two old snakes spent the winter on Holiday Hill. At the back of a crevice under some granite boulders there was an opening into an underground apartment. A woodchuck had dug this cave and used it as its first tenant, but it chanced to be vacant at the time and quite satisfactory to the Garters.

During the warmer midday hours of autumn Sir and Lady Garter often took sun baths in their hillside garden. From time to time other serpents of the same kind joined them, until at last there was a rather large house party of Garters.

They were all very fat and too lazy to go hunting. Their favorite amusement seemed to be basking in the sunshine. They did not allow themselves to become too heated; but they enjoyed having the temperature of their bodies raised a few degrees. Quite likely this was the best sort of way for them to pass the last pleasant fall days, for they would have no sunshine at all during the winter.

It was fortunate that these snakes were so sociable in the fall for, before really cold weather overtook them, all they needed to do was to retreat to cozy Woodchuck Den. This proved to be an excellent chamber for their winter rest.

They had a queer ceremony to perform while they were preparing for their long sleep. All the snakes twisted and curled and tied their bodies together into one big bundle of serpents.

This may not seem to you to be a comfortable resting position; but you have never taken the sort of sleep those snakes had. All through the coldest weather they did not yawn or stretch. They did not move. Looking at them very closely, you could not have seen that they were even breathing. They did not eat a mouthful; but their bodies were fat in the fall and thin in the spring, and so we may know that they were nourished by their own fat.

Such an almost breathless and almost foodless winter sleep, which certain animals take in cold climates, is called hibernation. Not all hibernating creatures rest in companies, as many seek solitary dens. Some, however, collect in bunches. And it is interesting to know that earthworms even tangle themselves into balls, a great many together. Being somewhat snakelike in shape, this is easy for them to do.

The warmth of spring wakened Sir and Lady Garter and all the others of the snake company. They came into the open and enjoyed the sunshine as much as they had enjoyed it in the fall.

But the snakes had somehow changed. They were not fat and lazy. They had lost their idle sociable house-party manners. After their long fast they needed food. They felt like hunting. And, after the manner of true hunters, they went forth alone.

Lady Garter slipped quietly along her solitary trail. Soon she found herself beyond the foot of the hill and at the edge of Holiday Meadow.

She stopped there for refreshments. For her spring breakfast she ate earthworms with pleasure. There is really nothing that tastes better to a half-starved garter snake than earthworms.

Of course frogs are good, too—hind legs and all! So it is not strange that she followed the stream along the meadow's edge and came to Holiday Pond, where larger game was abundant.

Lady Garter enjoyed the pond. She had not bathed all winter and her body felt very comfortable in the water. She soaked herself for some time. After she left her bath, she squeezed between two stones that were close together. As she pushed into the crevice she tore her skin near her jaws.

The edge of the pond was a pleasant hunting ground.

You need not feel sorry for Lady Garter. The torn place caused no pain. It was time for her to shed her skin. And thrusting her head between two rough stones was an easy way to begin to molt. It was not necessary to find a crevice at such times, but it was convenient.

After she had peeled her head, eyes and all, she crept on through the narrow place and freed herself of all her old thin skin, which she left behind her turned inside out like the finger of a tight glove.

The dry discarded molt did not remain long where it

was left beside the stones, however. A crested flycatcher was delighted to find it; for a bird of this kind never seems to be quite satisfied with her nest unless it has a good snake-skin lining.

Lady Garter was a handsome reptile in her fresh garment of scales. Her eyes were bright. Her back and sides were olive-brown with three long yellow stripes. The under part of her body was pale yellow with a tinge of green.

Her spring and early summer passed pleasantly enough. There was plenty to eat, and there were quiet places to rest. No exciting change came to her way of living until August when she found herself with a family of baby Garters.

Many kinds of snakes lay eggs which they leave for the warmth of the sun to hatch. But garter snakes do not lay their eggs. They keep them in their bodies until the little snakes inside all the eggs are fully formed. Then the young are born and they are able to run about at once.

Lady Garter's family of infant serpents numbered thirty-six. That was a moderate-sized family because sometimes garter snakes have fifty or sixty babies or even more.

Sir Talis and his thirty-five brothers and sisters were each about six inches long when they were born, and they grew rather fast because they ate so many nourishing earthworms.

All the young Garters could do their own hunting.

They even found their very first breakfast-worms for themselves. They were lively little things and enjoyed hunting for their food.

It was well for the mother that she did not need to pick up food and bring it to her three dozen youngsters. She had cares enough without attending to their diet of worms. For every time anything alarming happened, she was worried about her family.

She would lift her head and call "Hiss-iss-ss," and suddenly the young Garters would rush to their mother and almost immediately the whole family would be quite safe inside an underground den Lady Garter had chosen for her summer retreat.

Just how they all vanished so quickly and safely I, myself, never saw. During August and September I did not meet Lady Garter often enough for her to feel very well acquainted with me. There was always a stone or a bush or a hummock of grass between us. I never did get a clear view of that performance. So I have no records in my notebook about the mysterious disappearance of the Garter Family. I can only say that this is one of the wonderful ways of the serpent that I do not yet know.

The question is, after the mother snake lifted her head and gave her hissing call, did she hold her mouth open and did the little snakes rush into it? Did she then dart into the hole with them? Or did they merely run swiftly beside her and get into the hole that way?

Some people, who have written about garter snakes, have said that the mother snake never carries her very young babies to safety in her mouth and big stretchy throat. Would they, perhaps, have been wiser to say merely that they had never seen a garter snake do so?

For, on the other hand, some people who have watched very, very young garter snakes have a different sort of report to make. The most interesting account[2] I have ever read was written by an acquaintance of mine who has kindly given me permission to quote from it as follows:

"The country school in Iowa which the writer attended was held in the ordinary frame schoolhouse supported by a 'cobblestone' foundation of water-worn rocks more or less embedded in mortar. The schoolhouse faced the south and a set of narrow steps led up to the single central door. Through the foundation wall about halfway between these steps and the southeast corner of the building, and about eight to ten inches above the surface of the ground, was an irregular opening about two inches in diameter. This opening was used as a refuge one spring and summer by a large and 'motherly' looking specimen of the common garter snake of the region. The snake kept close to the hole at first and disappeared at the slightest sound. Later as we became interested in it, it was not disturbed and became accustomed to the ordinary noises of the children and would, if not too closely approached, often lie in the sun alongside the wall during recess time. One day as we came trooping out at noon the snake raised its head several inches from the ground and opened its mouth quite widely. This rather frightened us and all

2."Snakes 'Swallowing' Their Young," by E. D. Ball, *Iowa Academy of Science*, Vol. XXII, p. 343.

eyes were on the snake, when from around the corner of the house and from farther away in the yard came a number of small snakes which rushed pellmell into the mouth of the mother. When the last one was in, the mother snake raised her head quite high, wriggled over to the hole and disappeared. She was back there again the next recess and the performance was repeated for a number of days."

Sir Talis and his brothers and sisters kept within hearing of their mother's call during their first weeks. They came and stretched out beside her when they went to sleep.

The youngsters had a happy time that fall. They were peaceful, contented little serpents; and their affectionate mother guarded them so well when they were afraid that their courage soon came back to them.

They were even prettier than their mother while they were small. The dark olive color of their skin was a bit more greenish. Their narrow yellow stripes were clear and bright. And young snakes are much more slender and graceful than older ones.

Of course if you had seen Sir Talis just before one of his molting times, you would not have thought him to be very good-looking. His coat of scales was rather dull then. His eyes seemed whitish and he couldn't see very well.

When his eyes troubled him like that, he rubbed his head against a stone. After he was rid of the old skin on his head, it was rather easy for him to creep out of what was over the rest of his body. So, presently, there was Sir Talis again as fresh as new!

Like all Garters, Sir Talis was shy. If a person came near him, he usually slipped out of sight swiftly and quietly. He was not a coward, however, and stood his ground bravely enough if he were cornered. But in spite of his courage, he could not hurt even a child; so it was fortunate that the grown people and children of Holiday Farm were friendly to harmless kinds of snakes.

Sir Talis

Sir Talis had fine sharp teeth but there were no poison fangs in his mouth. His teeth were not for defense but to help him when he ate. They did not meet like chewing teeth but pointed inward. Since he could not chew he must swallow his food whole and the sharp slanting teeth helped push the food into his throat.

One of the queer ways of Sir Talis was that he could swallow a frog bigger than himself. His body walls stretched. He had an extra bone which hinged the upper jaw to the lower one and the jaws could spread wide apart. The two parts of his lower jaw could separate at the middle.

Thanks chiefly to earthworms and frogs, Sir Talis was fat before cold weather came. He felt rather lazy as he climbed Holiday Hill one day. He was glad to stop and join a Garter Party. Later, of course, he disappeared for the winter months, after the manner of his kind.

Perhaps you may meet him next spring while he is taking a sun bath on the hillside. And, as he vanishes among the rocks, you may think such swiftness in a creature with no feet is wonderful indeed. So it has seemed to wise men and poets. It was Emily Dickinson who wrote:

Yet when a child and barefoot, I more than once, at morn,
Have passed, I thought, a whiplash unbraided in the sun,
When, stooping to secure it, it wrinkled, and was gone.

The ribbon snake, a slender relative of the garter snake

CHAPTER VIII

THE VASE AND THE PLUME

Two trees stood well up on one side of Holiday Hill. Because of their shapes, they were called the Vase and the Plume. They were both the kind of tree that is known as the American Elm.

Other kinds of elm trees grow in America, too; but the name "American" has been given to the largest and most beautiful species we have in this country.

Years ago these trees were favorites with the people who came from England to settle in New England. Perhaps the newcomers brought with them an affection for elms because of the lovely elms of a different sort that they had left behind them across the sea.

So, to-day the branches of American elms meet in shady arches over the streets in some of our oldest cities. And their tall, straight trunks stand like stately columns before many of the oldest homes that white men built in our land. Old city streets and old dooryards are likely places to find such elm trees because they have been put there by the hands of men. But for countless centuries before men planted them, elm trees grew in rich soil near rivers. They grew, too, on hillsides, as they still do, in places where the ground is moistened by spring water. The wind scattered their seeds for them.

The Vase

An elm seed has a flat thin circular wrapper and a slender stem. The wrapper is green with a white fuzzy fringe around the edge. It is notched at one end.

Besides the brisk voyages which the breezes give the seeds, there are other ways in which the wind is helpful to elm trees. It even carries pollen for them.

As you know, pollen is needed by flowering plants. Their seeds cannot live without it. It forms on parts of the flowers that are called anthers. It is the duty of the dusty pollen to leave the anthers of one flower and find the sticky stigma in another flower. When a pollen grain reaches a ripe stigma, it grows like a tiny root and joins the seed to make it live.

Many kinds of plants have flowers with fragrance that insects can smell, colors that insects can see, and nectar that insects can drink. Such plants do not need wind to carry their pollen for them. Small messengers with wings attend to that ceremony.

Some kinds of plants, however, depend on wind at pollen times. Elms hang their anthers, like fringes, from their clustered blossoms. They swing in the air, and the breezes take the pollen and carry it away. Some of it is blown to other blossoming elm trees where the stigmas catch and use the grains of living dust.

Elm seeds take fluttery journeys by air.

Each spring the elm trees give their flowers the first right of way. The sap of growth rises and runs to the tip of every twig. But the leaves must all wait until the flowers have had their chance. If the leaves grew first, they would block the pollen traffic. Then the

Flower clusters of an elm tree

pollen grains would bump against the leaves and have accidents that would divert them from the direct air route from Station Anther to Station Stigma.

The trees cannot turn on red signal lights as warnings to the leaves that they must stop and wait before they cross the stage from brown buds to broad green bowers. But they have a strong law of nature that the leaves obey.

So it happened that the flowers on the Vase and the Plume had the branches and the breezes to themselves for a while. They were green and red and purple and they grew in pretty clusters. They gave the Vase the look of an enormous fountain with the branches and twigs for streams and sprays, and the flowers for mist. And they made the Plume seem very feathery indeed.

The days of the blossoms passed; and the flat-rimmed seeds had their turn with the wind; and at last the leaves unfolded.

Among the spring guests of the Vase and the Plume, were certain insects that selected their house lots there.

When one of these tapped the growing leaf with its beak, mysterious changes took place. On the flat green leafy door-yard, a marvelous little castle appeared.

An elm-leaf palace

If you should ask a scientist about such a structure, he would tell you, "That is a gall caused by an aphid." But a poet has said, "There is never a leaf nor a blade too mean to be some happy creature's palace!"

One day in May a gorgeous bird came to the Vase. His colors were black and flaming orange with some white and yellow. His early morning song sounded like a loud clear musical call.

The oriole's cradle

It may, indeed, have been a call. He had arrived in the North ahead of his mate. Perhaps she heard his voice as soon as she flew near Holiday Hill.

This much is certain—a pair of orioles had their nest fastened to a bough of the Vase that summer, and the wind rocked the baby birds while they were in their cradle.

Of all the guests that came to the Vase or the Plume, none was lovelier than Violet Tip. Who she was and what she did are related in another chapter. There is not really room in this one to tell even the names of all the visitors who used these trees for their summer camps. Nor were their boughs deserted during the winter.

In the fall the ripe leaves turned yellow and fluttered away—near or far, according to the strength of the gusty winds that scattered them. But hundreds of thousands of infant leaf buds remained—all bundled in shiny brown scales that they wore for winter suits. And near the spots where the stems of the old yellow leaves had let go their hold on the twigs, were the buds of next spring's flowers tucked close and snug in similar brown scales.

At last the Vase and the Plume were ready for their long winter rest. No butterfly floated near. No aphids dwelt in leafy palaces. But here and there, in one or another sheltering crevice, an insect slept—as egg or pupa or hibernating larva.

The orioles, old and young, were far away in some warm southern place. But hardier birds visited the elms. Woodpeckers tapped hopefully against the bark. On many a frosty morning, too, a little black-capped bird came to hunt for insect eggs for breakfast. He tilted this way and that among the twigs, like a performing acrobat. And the Chick-a-dee Song of this small bird was the cheeriest sound that could be heard on Holiday Hill in winter.

CHAPTER IX

PORT OF ELM

IF you were to take a journey through the waves of the summer wind far out into the sea of sunshine, what sort of sails would you choose?

Would you like the colors of one side to change, tint by tint, from creamy white to dark, rich brown— with a purple mist thrown over it and glistening silver marks in the middle? Would you like the other side to be bright brown, dappled with darker shades and tipped with dainty violet?

The wings of Violet Tip were like that, when she came sailing over Holiday Meadow one warm sunshiny day.

In that pleasant field were many plants that held sweet drops of nectar in their bright flower-cups. Violet Tip had often paused to sip from them on other voyages. The colors seemed to attract her, and she certainly liked the taste of nectar.

But this time she did not linger among the fragrant blossoms. She was sailing for another port. She was, indeed, taking the most important journey in the life of a butterfly.

Violet Tip

As Violet Tip drifted past the hedgerow that bordered the meadow, something caused her to change her course. She steered up the side of Holiday Hill.

Why should that little voyager turn away from the blossoms where she had often feasted? What was there in the air, that warm summer day, that seemed better to her than the fragrance of flowers? Who knows?

Perhaps, for once, an odor of leaves appealed to her more than the sweetness of flowers. It may be, for a time, that the scent of a plant belonging to the Nettle Family drew her. She, herself, had eaten many a green salad of such leaves. That, of course, was when she was young enough to have strong jaws instead of the long slender tongue that she now held coiled like a watch spring.

But what could she care about them now—nettles or hop or other leaves of that plant family? For on she went, straight up the hillside to a big elm tree, and there she stopped! And elms, as you may know, are closely related to nettles and hop—so closely, indeed, that many botanists say they belong to the Nettle Family.

What botanists say about elm trees did not concern Violet Tip. She had never seen a book about plants in her life. She did not need any person's advice about such matters. She had a surer guide to the plants than a book. Just what led her to an elm tree I cannot tell you. I think it was some odor; but, of course, I do not really know, because I have no way of learning how hop and nettles and elms smell to a butterfly.

This much, however, is certain. Violet Tip did steer straight for that tall tree, shaped like a great plume. She entered the Port of Elm, and there she stopped. While

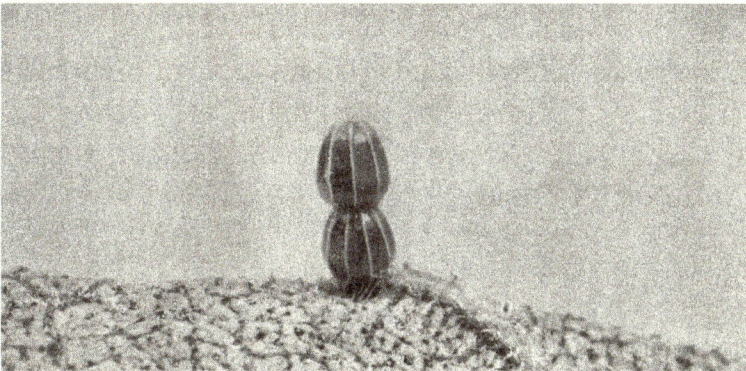

Two of Violet Tip's eggs—much enlarged

71

in that harbor, she anchored her eggs on some good fresh leaves, using a special sort of glue to hold them fast which would not melt in sunshine or dissolve in rain.

As soon as that important ceremony was over, Violet Tip lost her interest in elms or other members of the Nettle Family. She fluttered away in the sunshine; and, when she came to a gay fragrant blossom, she paused for refreshments. She uncoiled her tongue, and, dipping it into the tube of a flower, she sipped nectar as easily as you can suck lemonade through a straw.

One of Violet Tip's names was Grapta. So that is what we may as well call the daughter-caterpillar that was in one of the eggs that had been put on the elm leaves. The egg was lovely as a tiny green jewel. It was almost barrel-shaped, and it had ridges and delicate white creases.

The weather was warm and baby Grapta stayed inside the pretty eggshell for only four days. Then she nibbled a hole in the top of her thin barrel and poked

Grapta hatched from one of Violet Tip's eggs
and grew to be a spiny caterpillar.

out her shiny bald head. She had a droll way of nodding it as she crept over the ragged edge.

A taste of eggshell seemed all right for part of her breakfast; but very soon the baby caterpillar was ready for something more nourishing. There was nothing anywhere near Grapta except elm leaves—elm leaves beneath her, elm leaves above her, elm leaves on every side of her. However, that was just the food Grapta needed for the present. Such a diet agreed with her quite as well as a menu of hop or nettle or other closely related plants.

Violet Tip and her brothers and sisters
had eaten elm-leaf salads.

Like all growing caterpillars, Grapta molted her skin several times. The outer covering of her head came off and she got rid of even the lining of her breathing tubes. Of course new ones grew. She could not eat for a few hours before she molted. Her jaws would not work. And I suppose she had no appetite. But each time she shed her skin her mouth became larger than before and she could eat faster.

Her last caterpillar-suit was quite different from her first one. Its color was brown with many fine white markings. It was covered with rows of branched spines.

After Grapta grew to be as large as a caterpillar of her kind can be, she spun some silk. Most caterpillar silk is white or cream-colored or gray or brown. But Grapta's silk was pink—rather a bright pink, too.

She did not make a cocoon with her silk fibers. She spun and wove a thin pad on the underside of an elm twig. She put a tuft of silk near the center of the pad.

Grapta was a natural acrobat. She took hold of this silk tuft with her hind feet and then swung head down. She did this the first time she tried.

While she was hanging in this position a change was going on inside her spiny coat. Several hours later this old garment ripped; and quite a different Grapta wriggled out of it. There was no longer a caterpillar hanging from the silk tuft. The object that was there was a chrysalis.

Grapta certainly had a queer shape while she was in this stage. One end of her body looked like a head with two stiff horns and a big Roman nose. The other part had bright spots that looked like gold and silver and rows of little spikes.

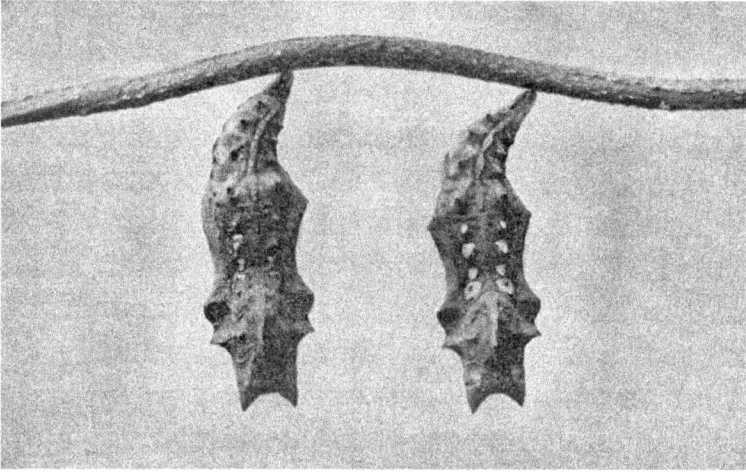

Grapta and one of her sisters when they were chrysalises

After staying inside her chrysalis case for nearly two weeks, Grapta broke this thin covering and crept out of it. Of course this time she was a butterfly. She felt no interest at all in elm leaves. A new world lay before her. She faced a flood of sunshine through which breezes brought the fragrance of flowers. Gradually her wings stretched out like lovely brown sails with violet tips.

You will not be surprised by what Grapta did next. She left the bough of that great elm which had been her safe harbor (through egg-days and larva-days and pupa-days); and drifted away to the glorious goldenrod islands where she drank the first nectar she had ever tasted.

When the autumn days grew cool, Grapta sought a

nook where she might rest long and quietly.

Like Rana the yelping frog, and Lotor the raccoon, and Whistling Wejack the woodchuck, and Sir Talis the serpent, Grapta, the frail violet-tipped butterfly, passed the cold winter weeks in that strange sleep that is called hibernation.

The sunshine of springtime wakened her before the plants had their nectar ready to serve. But Grapta did not go hungry. Sap, leaking from bruised bark on oaks and other trees, had a savory tang. And before many days some early spring blossoms held their cups of nectar for her and other thirsty insects.

But at last there came a day, as there had come to her mother, when her own hunger and thirst were forgotten. She turned away from the fragrance of flowers and their sweet juices. A most important journey lay before her. She needed no map or compass to show her the way. As thousands of generations of violet-tipped butterflies had done before her, Grapta set sail for the good old Port of Elm.

CHAPTER X

JUNCO

JUNCO's feather coat and hood were the color of slate, and his feather vest was white. There was nothing really showy about this neat dark gray and white bird unless it was his tail. His central tail-feathers were dark slate or sooty-colored, nearly black, and his outer tail-feathers were white. When he flew, he showed the white margins of his tail in rather a flashy way.

Junco spent most of the year on Holiday Hill near a clump of evergreen trees. These stood on a part of the hill where no fires had burned for many years and they had had a good chance to grow tall and spread their broad branches.

Not far from these trees was a bubbling spring. The water that flowed from it was so cold that the ground near it was cool even on the hottest summer days.

It was, perhaps, because of the trees and the spring that Junco stayed on Holiday Hill, for he liked cool places. If he had not found a comfortable spot on that hill he probably would have gone elsewhere. He might have traveled to the edge of some forest far to the north.

Or, after he had flown about a hundred miles away, he might have found a hill high enough to be called a mountain. And there, near the snow that capped the mountain even in summer, he might have chosen to stay.

Junco

However, as it was, Junco was quite happy on Holiday Hill. It was easy for him to find plenty of food there, and good things to eat helped to keep him contented. He liked blueberries; and for about eight weeks, he could pick all he wished of these round juicy fruits.

Junco needed meat, too, and he hunted for it himself. He went here and there on his hunting trips so that he led rather an active life.

There were some little queer-shaped, long-snouted beetles, called weevils, that had a very good flavor; and Junco flew to the tops of some pine trees when he was hungry for them.

These weevils laid their eggs in the growing tips of pine trees. The young that hatched from their eggs were small grubs that ate the inside parts of the top, or leading, pine shoots. Of course such grubs were not good for the pines. So the more of the beetles Junco could catch before they laid their eggs, the better for these lovely trees.

It was Junco who helped take care of the pine that grew in a crack in the top of a great boulder. On many a morning, while the day was still cool, he hunted among the branches at the top of that tree and often found a weevil there for a part of his breakfast.

Junco did a great deal for the blueberries, too. There were several sorts of beetles and many kinds of caterpillars and various other insects that fed on the leaves or the fruit of these bushes. Junco captured hundreds of these and so earned his fruit while he hunted for his meat.

Of course the little gray and white bird did not reason about his food. He simply swallowed whatever tasted good to him. He did not know that there would be more berries if he ate the insects he found on the bushes. But Uncle David understood what Junco and the other birds were doing, and welcomed them in his fields.

He often said to whichever niece or nephew happened to be visiting Holiday Farm: "The birds help take care of the berry crop. So it is only fair that they should have part of the berries to eat. They are working for their board."

Plenty of food and a comfortable climate were good for Junco's health. But they would not have been enough, just in themselves, to keep him as happy as he was. He needed companionship, too, for he was a sociable, affectionate little chap; and it really would have been a pity if he had had a lonely life.

So you will be glad to learn that another bird was often with Junco on his hillside picnics and hunting trips. She wore a feather suit very much like his, though the gray parts were not so dark. Since she was his mate, we may call her Mrs. Junco.

Just what Junco called her, I cannot tell you, for he did not use words when he spoke to her. At least he did not use any words that human beings can understand. But each bird made queer little chirps and clinking sounds which must have meant something to the other.

Perhaps, when he chirped one way, he was asking, "Where are you?" It may be that her answering notes were to say, "I'm over here, now."

It seems likely enough that another sort of chatter may have been Junco's manner of calling: "Oh, I'm having the most delightful luck with my hunting! Come

Mrs. Junco

and see what I'm finding and catch some, too."

And I think her cheerful reply may have meant something like "I'm on my way," because she flew over to join Junco at once, displaying her white tail-feathers as she went.

Then there were Junco's warbles which were so soft and gentle that they seemed like sweet whispered bits of songs. What did they mean? Perhaps, nothing at all; except that he was so very happy that he simply could not keep still!

In May, the two Juncos hunted for something besides food. They looked for the best place on the hill for a nest. The spot they chose was a bit of ground not far from the cold spring and the clump of evergreens.

The birds were quite busy for several mornings building the nest. They made the outer frame of shreds of bark and little roots and old grass. For a lining they gathered softer pieces of the same sort which they used with some hair they were fortunate enough to find.

The slanting side of a rock leaned over their little house lot and sheltered the nest. In this pleasant nook Mrs. Junco spent most of her time for a while.

Soon after the nest was finished she laid an egg in it. The eggshell was bluish white, prettily marked with different shades of purple and brown. Some of the dark blotches formed a little wreath about the larger end of the egg.

Mrs. Junco laid one egg each day until there were five of the dainty things in the nest. Then she began keeping them warm by sitting on them so that they were covered by her soft under feathers. She stayed there most of the time, herself, though now and then Mr. Junco guarded the nest while she went away for a little change. At such times she took a drink at the spring and found some food; but she did not leave her eggs very long.

After nearly twelve days the baby birds that had been growing all the time inside of the lovely shells were large and strong enough to hatch. They were queer-looking little things until their feathers grew.

These five young Juncos were so hungry that their father and mother did not have much time for rest, except at night, until the babies were old enough to leave the nest and hunt for themselves. A diet of insects was better than any other food for the growing youngsters; and you may be sure that Mr. and Mrs. Junco had many lively hours finding enough to put into those gaping mouths.

Of course the Juncos were as quiet and careful as possible when they were flying to and from their nest. But one day two girls happened to find the secret place. These cousins came to the spring for a drink—and there on a near-by branch was Mrs. Junco with her bill full of insects.

However, these children knew what to do. They slipped out of sight among some bushes to hide. They were so still that after a few minutes Mrs. Junco felt that it was safe to visit her nest and feed her young.

It was a bit surprising to see how the young birds differed from the old Juncos. Even after their feathers were grown and they were leaving their nest, they did not look the same. For where the old birds were slate-colored, the youngsters were grayish brown and pale buff. And they were spotted and streaked with dark or blackish marks above and below.

However, before winter the young birds shed their baby feathers. In their second suits they looked much like their father and mother. They had lost their dark spots and streaks, though they were still rather brown.

During the fall days when bright leaves were

dropping from the trees, juncos that had nested in far northern places traveled southward. Some stopped in southern New England and some went much farther.

The Juncos of Holiday Hill, however, did not spend their winter in the South. They did not, indeed, go more than a short flight from their summer home.

In the hedge that bordered the meadow, at the foot of the hill, were some evergreen trees in a more sheltered place than those on the slope. Here the Junco family often spent the night. They found seeds for breakfast and some for other meals on the plants near the meadow.

One morning when they woke they looked upon a strange world. The hill was a great white mound. The field, too, had become white in the night. Piles of fluffy white stuff lay on the pine boughs about them.

The young birds had never seen snow before. They did not seem to mind the cold weather; but it was hard for them to find seeds when there was so much snow in the way.

But Mr. and Mrs. Junco had both seen the snows of more than one winter. They flew here and there and called cheerfully when they came to some weedy tips which held their seeds above the snow. Then, suddenly, they seemed to remember something pleasant. Perhaps the snow reminded them. For on many a snowy morning, the winter before, they had found plenty of seeds quite easily.

They flew to the barns of Holiday Farm, and the

young birds went with them. There on the floor of an open shed they found a lot of soft bits that had been swept from the hayloft and scattered in the shed. In the midst of this dry stuff was a handful of clover seeds. A little to one side lay a heap of sand and fine gravel.

Junco and his family did not know how their winter breakfast happened to be spread in this convenient place. They ate what they needed and flew away. Then they came again when they wished another meal, just as they had been going to the seedy outdoor places before the snow fell. They were very cheerful when they visited the shed and chattered cozily over their food.

No, the hungry birds did not know who swept the broken bits from the hayloft and brought fresh seeds and fine gravel so that there was always enough each day. But four young people who were spending the winter with Uncle David knew all about it.

And, perhaps, it would be hard to tell whether the birds had a happier time eating their treats than the children of Holiday Farm had while they scattered the seeds or watched their cheery feathered guests.

CHAPTER XI

LITTLE SNOWSHOES

HOLIDAY HILL was white with snow. The light from the full moon was so bright that there were dark blue shadows under the tamarack trees.

These trees were growing on a boggy part of the hill. In summer, tufts of fine leaves were like lovely short green tassels on their branches. Near them stood many soppy little green sedge hummocks. Tree trunks that had fallen there were covered with velvety green moss.

But that shining winter night the tamarack grove was not green. The open brown cones on their branches showed that they were related to pine and spruce and fir and other cone-bearing trees. But, unlike other members of the Pine Family, the tamaracks were not evergreens. Their leaves had turned yellow in the fall and had dropped to the ground, where they now lay deep under the snow which covered also the sedgy tussocks and the mossy logs.

If you had tried to walk up the hill you would have found yourself knee-deep in the soft snow, for there was no hard crust to walk on. That is, you would have been wading unless you had put on snowshoes.

The white rabbit who came out of the tamarack grove wore snowshoes on his hind feet. Of course he had not strapped them on as a person does. His snowshoes grew where he needed them.

His hind feet were large at all times of the year. And in winter his long spreading toes were covered with especially thick hair which formed a broad pad on each hind foot. With feet of this sort he could go easily over the snow even when it was soft instead of crusty.

The ground was white with snow.

Little Snowshoes in his winter furs

It was important for the white rabbit, or Little Snowshoes as we may call him, to be able to travel on the snow. How else was he to find food in winter?

He had not put away a harvest of cones as Chickaree, the squirrel, had done. He had not stuffed his skin with fat, in preparation for a long foodless sleep after the manner of Wejack, the woodchuck, or Sir Talis, the serpent. When he was hungry he must go in search of something to eat.

It may seem to you like a cheerless and chilly errand to go out at night, no matter how cold the weather, to get your own food and eat it alone on a frozen hillside.

But Little Snowshoes did not mind. He liked his evening picnics all by himself. It was only a few hops from the tamarack grove to a growth of young birches and poplars.

There had once been large trees of these kinds on ground that was not so wet as that where the tamaracks stood. The old trees had been cut and the new ones were more like bushes growing in thick clumps.

The white rabbit was glad to wander through those bushes. He felt at home among them. It was easy to hide there. And he could always find plenty of his favorite food.

For Little Snowshoes was fond of birch and poplar bark. His teeth were just the right sort to use for paring it off the stems. Of course a stem could not grow if its bark was cut off. In some places this might have been a serious matter. But Little Snowshoes did not worry about that. Neither did anyone else. Indeed, Uncle David, down at Holiday Farm, said that the rabbit helped keep the birches from growing large enough to shade the blueberries too much.

As there were always plenty of smaller birches and poplars growing in the summer to take the places of those that had been chewed, Little Snowshoes had good bark to eat each winter. When there was only a little snow on the ground, the white rabbit ate the bark on the lower part of the stems. When the snow was deep, he went out on his snowshoes and peeled the bark from the higher places.

Being white, Little Snowshoes did not show much on the snow. He usually stayed in sheltered places during the day and rested. If he saw a dog or a fox, or if he heard any sound that worried him, he kept as motionless as a hump of snow. That was an excellent way for a white creature to hide. Evening and night and very early morning were the times he chose for his rambles and his picnic luncheons.

If you find the tracks of such a rabbit along the margin of some low swamp trees or on a boggy hillside, you can tell what kind of animal made them by their shape. You can know they are made by a snowshoe rabbit because the prints of his hind feet are so very large.

Of course the marks of his big feet will be ahead of those of his small front feet.

If you wish to know how he gets them that way, perhaps you can find the reason by watching a rabbit when he hops!

The cold season passed quietly and pleasantly enough for the solitary white rabbit. One night when it was nearly spring, Little Snowshoes heard a noise near his camping ground, a muffled thump-thump-thump which sounded almost like the beating of a queer drum. It came through the air in dull booms. It made the ground tremble slightly.

To Little Snowshoes that sound was a challenge. A

stranger rabbit had entered his yard and was knocking to announce his arrival. Little Snowshoes answered him. He used his strong hind legs as drumsticks. He let the ground under him serve as a drum. When he pounded there was a dull, rapid thump-thump-thump that sounded through the air and quivered through the ground.

Then Little Snowshoes went to meet his uninvited guest. He did not feel neighborly toward him. He could not speak in words. He could not say: "Go away! You are not welcome here." But, in a manner known to rabbits, he made himself understood. The newcomer was disappointed. But he hopped away.

The next night another rabbit came and pounded upon the ground near Little Snowshoes. He, too, departed without being invited to a picnic meal.

But one night in early March a rabbit came who felt no fear of Little Snowshoes. She heard him drumming and liked his tune. She was timid in many ways, but the thump of a rabbit's feet was pleasant for her to hear.

One name of this rabbit was Wabasso. You may have read, in another book, how

> the rabbit, the Wabasso,
> Sat upright to look and listen.

That is what this Wabasso did when she heard Little Snowshoes drum. Then she went, calmly enough, into his camping ground and stayed there. Little Snowshoes did not try to frighten her away. He liked her and she became Mrs. Wabasso Snowshoes.

Little Snowshoes and Wabasso in winter furs

If you had met these two rabbits near the tamaracks some moonlight night in April, they would have stood quite still. Do you think you could have seen them, white as snow, against the dark ground? Not at all. These rabbits were not white in April. They were brown. They had molted their thick winter coats and grown their summer furs. Their hind feet were still large and their toes were long and spreading; but their broad hairy snowshoe-like pads were gone for the summer.

So you see the reason why rabbits like Little Snowshoes and Wabasso are called "varying hares."

Little Snowshoes in summer furs

Later that spring Wabasso made a nest in a sheltered place under a heap of old birch branches. She brought some straw and dry brown leaves for the outside of the nest. She lined the hollow with downy fur which she pulled from her breast.

In this soft nest her five little sons and daughters were born. But they did not stay there long. Their mother gave them plenty of milk to drink. So they grew very fast and were soon able to hop here and there and find tender juicy plants to eat.

During the day the baby rabbits rested. By the time

night came they were wide awake and ready for picnics and frolics. They were sociable youngsters and jolly playmates. They drummed on the ground with their hind feet, but their thumps were only in fun. They had a game of leaping over one another which they seemed to enjoy like a merry joke.

The young rabbits were brown that summer and early fall. But, by the time the ground was covered with snow, they were wearing white winter furs. They had on their warm coats and their broad snowshoes when they hopped in the moonlight on Christmas Eve and feasted on delicious birch bark.

www.ingramcontent.com/pod-product-compliance
Lightning Source LLC
Chambersburg PA
CBHW032021090426

42741CB00006B/693